THE
RIGHT TO STRIKE

Prepared by the Working Party on
HUMAN RIGHTS
established by the
BISHOPS' CONFERENCE
OF ENGLAND AND WALES

CATHOLIC TRUTH SOCIETY
Publishers to the Holy See
38/40 ECCLESTON SQUARE
LONDON SW1V 1PD

Published by
The Incorporated Catholic Truth Society, London

ISBN 0 85183 283 0

PUBLISHED BY THE INCORPORATED CATHOLIC TRUTH SOCIETY, LONDON
AND PRINTED BY THE BURLEIGH PRESS, FISHPONDS, BRISTOL
Printed in England   *August,* 1979
RJC

CONTENTS

* * *

FOREWORD

This pamphlet is a statement for discussion. It is intended to give the reader an idea of the main questions and problems, and to point the way to some possible answers. It does *not* provide 'the' answer to any of these important and difficult problems. That is because different people may give varying weight to the moral issues involved, and because different solutions may be equally possible and desirable.

The Statement has been prepared by a group of people, some with legal experience, some with a special interest in issues of morality; but none has had any special experience in industrial relations. We are aware that there are aspects which we may have missed or misunderstood; but we give the results of where our discussions and thinking have led us so far. We offer this Statement to our readers very tentatively, in the hope that it will provoke further conscientious and constructive discussion, inside the Church as well as outside it.

As for the more purely legal parts of the Statement, both

about the current law of this country and about our international obligations and the human rights which they protect, we hope that the reader will find these useful summaries.

As the statement is tentative, a sort of 'Green Paper' and no more, we must stress two things: first, not every individual member of the Working Party necessarily subscribes to every suggestion or assessment in it (though the Statement represents a general and provisional consensus to which we have come); and secondly, it is issued by the members of the Working Party who sign below *in their individual capacities*. Nothing in this Statement must be taken to represent the views of the Bishops of England and Wales, who have yet to express a collective opinion on this subject.

The Statement was partly prepared before the industrial troubles of the Spring of this year; but we believe that those troubles confirmed rather than disproved our analysis of the problems.

We express our warm thanks to those who have helped with advice at different stages of our work, and notably Professor Cyril Grunfeld, John Harriott, Joe Kirwan and Professor B. A. Wortley, Q.C. Again we emphasise that none of these should be taken to subscribe to any particular statement of fact or opinion contained in the pamphlet.

> The Rt Revd Bishop Basil Christopher Butler, OSB
> The Rt Revd Bishop Gerald Moverley
> Professor A. N. Allott (*Chairman*)
> Mrs Kathleen Baxter
> The Revd Dr Gerard Hughes, SJ
> The Revd Robert Ombres, OP (*Secretary*)
> Michael Penty, Esq.
> Paul Sieghart, Esq.
> Sir Francis Vallat

THE RIGHT TO STRIKE
A Statement for Discussion

Prepared by the Working Party on Human Rights established by the Bishops' Conference of England and Wales.

PART ONE

AN EXPLANATION OF THE PROBLEMS

Has morality anything to do with strikes?

1. 'A mass strike forced a major London hospital to close its doors to all new patients this afternoon. . . . We have cancelled all admissions, even urgent ones (said the hospital administrator). Our sterile supply department is out on strike and there is only a short space of time before we start to run out of dressings.'

    (Report in London *Evening Standard*, 19 October 1978**)**

    Regrettably this is only one of many major, and countless minor, strikes which have hit the care and treatment of patients in hospitals. Strikes (and other 'industrial action') affecting the health service are merely an extreme example of the use of an industrial weapon to achieve some end seen as desirable by workers, union leaders, or shop stewards in a particular place of employment. And when we speak of 'workers', it is important to note that it is not only the lower-paid 'blue-collar' employees that are referred to; highly paid doctors, civil servants, and managers of industrial enterprises are themselves workers and may resort to industrial action to press their claims for higher pay or status. The confrontation, therefore, is no longer between poor and rich. Throughout this Statement, 'worker' should therefore be read in this broader sense.

2. Public reaction to strikes threatening essential services

such as fire prevention, hospital treatment, or the supply of electricity to houses, is often extremely hostile: to some it may seem like an abuse of monopoly power. Many other strikes, like those in the motor industry, do not prompt the same hostile reaction; but they are often widely condemned as irresponsible or greedy. A strike may have a straightforward motive, such as a demand for higher wages or better conditions; or it may be a dispute between different unions for the exclusive right to recruit; or it may be provoked by a desire to exclude non-union labour; or it may be over differentials; or it may be in support of some other industrial dispute elsewhere; or it may be for some non-industrial end.

3. There are, however, two sides to the picture. Despite the frequently hostile reaction from the public, those who call strikes, and often those who strike, genuinely assume that they have a legitimate cause for striking. And yet those who follow a strike call out of solidarity, or even out of fear of the consequences, may sometimes wonder in their heart of hearts whether all strikes, or this particular strike, can be justified, that is, be just and moral. The employee on strike may stifle his doubts; seeing that industrial disputes are almost entirely removed these days from the control of the law in the United Kingdom, he or she may conclude that they are effectively outside the sphere of morality as well. If the law doesn't prevent it, it must be permissible.

4. But is this right? The hospital administrator in the instance we started with is reported as saying:

'The view of the medical and nursing staff is that this strike is putting patients at risk. How can this be justified?'

A member of his staff remarked that:

'This is a group of militant trade unionists who are hijacking the hospital.'

4

The strike-leader, a shop steward, commented:
> 'I feel very sorry that the hospital has closed to all admissions but it is not our fault.'

5. Up till now, there has been no clear and adequate guide available to Christians, or indeed to anyone with a conscientious concern with justice, by which they can decide for themselves when a strike may be just. Our Statement tries to remedy this lack by setting out principles by which to judge whether any particular strike, or other type of industrial action, is morally justifiable. To do this, we must discover the *main issues* involved, legal and economic as well as moral, the *principles* of right action which apply to man's life in community with his fellows, and the *questions* which every person must put to himself if called upon to take part in industrial action or to judge the morality of action taken by others.

6. What we cannot do is to supply all the answers. Particular cases are often not as black and white as they are painted; legitimate grievances and legitimate claims may only be seen for what they are by people with a first-hand knowledge of the circumstances; it may, or again it may not, be true that the withdrawal of labour is the only way of making them known and getting them remedied; only those closely in touch with the problem may be in a position to tell. But while we cannot supply answers, we can insist that the issues involved are moral issues. The conscientious individual, having weighed all the facts, applied all the principles, and sought an answer to all the questions, must see that the decision he then faces is a moral one. He cannot simply take refuge in the idea that 'I must strike with my mates', or seek to evade responsibility for the consequences of his decision by saying 'It is not our fault'. He *is* responsible for what he decides to do.

7. It is important to emphasise that there are two sides to industrial relations, and two sides to industrial action. An

obvious point, perhaps, but in considering the morality of workers withdrawing their labour one must not forget the equal gravity of the responsibility of the employer. 'Industrial action' includes action by an employer; and the effects of such action as a mass lockout or termination of employment, whether due to redundancy or not, may be as severe as any strike. Employers must therefore reflect with equal caution before inflicting such action on employees. Management too have duties, not merely to abstain from such action where it cannot be morally justified, but to provide conditions of work and openness to complaints about conditions from their employees which will help to forestall industrial action to remedy such complaints. However, this is a statement about the 'right to strike'; and it would complicate our task and prolong the statement if we discussed this other set of questions in detail now. We must therefore content ourselves with a reminder that the duties on employers are an equally important subject which will merit future consideration.

The diversity of 'strikes'
8.   Part of the difficulty is that there is no single form of strike; instead, there are many *types* of 'industrial action'; the *go-slow* and *work-to-rule*; the *sit-in*; '*sending an individual to Coventry*' or '*blacking*' a firm; the *sympathetic strike*; the *boycott* or *blacking* of another enterprise or its goods; as well as the straightforward downing of tools and walking off the job. The euphemism 'industrial action' is found convenient by those who resort to it, as it neutralises and removes any moral opprobrium from the action and its consequences. In reality, of course, industrial action, other than picketing, is often *inaction*, not doing something. In a liberal society it is easier to stop people doing things, whether by law or physical control, than to cause them to do things they do not want to do – hence

6

the effectiveness of so much industrial action.

9.   Strikes and other forms of industrial action are as diverse in their *causes* as in their forms. These have already been mentioned in para. 2. We shall have to consider (in Part Four) whether there are legitimate and illegitimate grounds for striking. In the particular instance we started with, the strike seems to have had its roots in the procedures adopted for detecting stealing by hospital staff; but thereafter the cause of the prolongation of the strike was stated to be the lack of consultation, by the management, of one union about the lifting of suspension on an employee not a member of that union. Resentment at investigation of alleged crimes by employees, and assertion of union power to control hiring and firing, are thus two further causes to add to our list. The example also shows how quickly a strike acquires a multiple causation: the original source of grievance is replaced or added to by other new grievances.

Is there a 'right' to strike?

10.   Those who seek to justify a particular strike often do so by invoking the 'right to strike'. This is seen as a fundamental right of every worker. *Right* is a tricky word: it can mean

(i) **a claim guaranteed by the law** of a particular country, defined by that law and protected by it;

(ii) **a basic entitlement** of every human being under a higher law -- a divine law, or the natural law, or the internationally recognised code of fundamental human rights;

(iii) **a claim grounded in social morality** by one person against the fellow-members of the country or society to which he belongs.

11.   In Part Three of this Statement we look briefly at the law of this country, and see how far it defines and protects

the right to strike. We also look at how far the law protects persons from the harmful consequences of the exercise by others of their right or power to strike. Legal rights, as we shall see, do not play an important part in resolving our problem – at least in this country.

12.   We are members of a Working Party on Human Rights. It is because of this that we are especially concerned with the recognition or non-recognition of a fundamental human right to strike. This also we discuss in Part Three. At this point we need only mention that while the right to strike is fundamental to a free society the *right not to strike*, and the *right not to be injured by a strike*, may also be fundamental rights calling for examination and protection.

13.   The rights and wrongs of strikes in the ethical or moral sense are the main concern of this Statement. We set them out and discuss them in Part Four.

Terminology

14.   It is impossible to discuss these issues without using the appropriate specialised terms. We have tried to keep technical vocabulary to a minimum consistent with clarity. But the law is full of technical terms, naturally; so indeed are ethical theory, moral theology, and economic science. A frequent source of confusion is the use by different experts of the same words in different ways and with different meanings: thus 'right' and 'obligation' have technical meanings for the lawyer which may be different from those used by the moralist.

To avoid confusion, this Statement will use the expression 'legal right' when what is meant is 'right' in the first sense mentioned in para. 10; that is, a claim guaranteed by the law of a particular country. 'Legal right' may include, where appropriate, legal privileges, powers and immunities. 'Right' without qualification means a right not necessarily recognised by law, an ethical right or social right. 'Legal duty', 'legal obligation', etc., are used similarly.

15. 'Strike' may be used in this Statement as shorthand for strikes and other forms of industrial action, where no confusion can be caused by so doing. To speak technically, a strike is a withdrawal of labour by an employee, usually in concert with other employees, and usually in breach of his contract of employment, in order to obtain some advantage from or procure some course of action by his employer. If the withdrawal of labour is not in breach of the employee's contract, then it may be, with exceptions, morally justifiable; so that in practice our examination of the morality of strikes will go beyond those strikes which are in breach of contract, and will also cover those which are in breach of (usually non-enforceable) agreements between management and labour about conditions of work. A withdrawal or denial of labour, even where there is no agreement, legal or otherwise, may be equally open to criticism on ethical grounds, and will therefore have to be included in our Statement. Many other forms of industrial action, e.g., the go-slow, though not being a complete withdrawal of labour, may be in breach of contract under common law; the work-to-rule, though purporting to be a scrupulous performance of the employment contract, may well also in practice be in breach of it or of implied terms in it.

A disclaimer

16. To discuss industrial action and its legitimacy is already a major undertaking. We understand very well that this subject is only part of, and dependent on, the whole scheme of industrial relations; while industrial relations in their turn are merely part of the way in which the economic life of the country is carried on. A full critique of striking should thus involve a reference to industrial relations, to economics, and to politics and the social order generally.

9

We cannot possibly undertake all this in the compass of a short Statement on the right to strike; nor would it add to its usefulness for the ordinary reader if we tried to.

17. But, for the removal of doubts, we must emphasise that we do not criticise, and fully accept:

    (i) the right of persons to work or not to work;

    (ii) the legitimacy and value of trade unions;

    (iii) the need to look at society, and social relations, as a whole when evaluating any segment of it.

18. We also accept that the conditions, problems and attitudes of the present cannot be properly understood, or fairly judged, without regard to the historical experiences and processes which have brought them into being. That is why Part Two deals briefly with the historical background to industrial relations and the use of the strike weapon in this country. Each nation is a unique case; the principles to be applied may be universal, but the circumstances of their application, and the context in which they have to operate, are peculiar and special to each country.

19. Lastly, a verbal point. Because of the exigencies of English grammar, we have used 'he' and 'his' in talking of the worker throughout; but we naturally have the position and interests of female workers equally in mind, and what we say is intended to apply to them just as much as to their male colleagues.

PART TWO

THE HISTORICAL BACKGROUND

1. As we shall see, workers in Britain today have a statutory right to organise themselves into trade unions for the representation of their interests; and these unions are in such a powerful position, both in social fact and in the eyes of the law, that they are virtually immune from any sort of control by the law.

What is more, though workers do not in a formal sense have a legal right to strike, if they do decide to strike they will be largely immune from legal responsibility for the consequences of their actions, except in so far as their contract with their employers is concerned.

2. Was it always so? Far from it – working men (and women) in Britain had to battle hard and long to establish their right to form trade unions. Many features of their employment in the old days – the long hours, the low wages, the constant threat of dismissal, insanitary and unsafe conditions of work, dictatorial supervision – strike the modern mind as shameful, so that the necessity for workers to be able to organise and defend themselves against powerful employers was clearly there. Nevertheless, the law in the beginning treated trade unions as unlawful combinations and those who formed them were liable to severe punishment.

It was the same with the 'right to strike'. Workers who agreed to withdraw their labour, even for an apparently legitimate end, were liable to be prosecuted and punished for a criminal conspiracy.

3. The starting point of our investigation, and its history for many years thereafter, was marked by strife, bitterness, and the repeated use of the law to smash workers' trade unions and later to frustrate their use of the right to with-

draw their labour. This history of bitterness, aggravated by the facts and the mythology of the General Strike of 1926 (as sharp a turning point in industrial relations as the Great War had been in international relations only a few years before), explains the Them and Us mentality of industrial relations, the atmosphere of conflict, the distrust and hostility shown to all attempts to control or eliminate industrial conflicts by the use of the law.

4. We have inherited this legacy of bitterness, confrontation and conflict; and, in addition, organised and even unorganised workers have, since the Second World War, become gradually more aware of their industrial strength. The complexity of the modern economy; full or overfull employment leading to shortage of labour; the cost of modern industrial investment in factories, equipment and processes; the arrival of governments too weak or too acquiescent to moderate the excesses of union power – such are the main causes which aided this development. Just as with the colonial peoples, who threw off colonial rule as soon as they realised their own strength and the weakness of opposition to their claims for independence, so in the industrial sphere consciousness of worker-power and the readiness to exploit it were fed by the obvious weakness of employers and governments.

Trade unions

5. Statutory wage and price control in England goes back many centuries, to the first Statute of Labourers 1349. It was thereafter a criminal offence to demand, or to organise to demand, higher wages. The Combination Acts of 1799 and 1800 effectively made combinations of workmen into criminal conspiracies. But surprisingly early, in 1824, the Acts were repealed, and trade unions ceased to be illegal organisations. However, workers who combined to injure someone else might be, and often were, prosecuted for a

criminal conspiracy after 1824. The Trade Union Act 1871 made formal provision for trade unions, including their recognition and the necessity for them to have written rules.

The Conspiracy and Protection of Property Act 1875 greatly extended the immunities of striking workers and their unions, by providing that two or more persons could not be indicted for a criminal conspiracy to do an act '*in contemplation or furtherance of a trade dispute*', if the act itself was not criminal. These are hallowed words in British industrial relations law, and are still with us.*

6. Criminal conspiracy was now largely eliminated as a weapon to use against workers and their unions who concertedly withdrew their labour for industrial ends. Instead there was recourse to the civil law of conspiracy, and many successful actions in tort were brought for damages and injunctions. The famous *Taff Vale* case† established that a registered trade union was liable to pay damages for torts committed by its members acting on its behalf. The Trade Disputes Act 1906 was passed largely to remedy the results of this decision.

By the Act, immunity in tort was given to one who caused economic harm to another by inducing a third party to break his contract of employment with that person, provided it was done in contemplation or furtherance of a trade dispute. In addition, a blanket immunity in tort was conferred on the trade union as such. These principles were re-affirmed in the Trade Union and Labour Relations Acts 1974–76. Indeed, the immunity for, in effect, trade union officials was extended to secondary boycotts and 'blacking' generally by immunising from legal action any person who caused economic harm to another by inducing

* See, for example, the Trade Union and Labour Relations Acts 1974-76.
† *Taff Vale Railway* v. *Amalgamated Society of Railway Servants* [1901] A.C. 426.

a third party to break any kind of contract, commercial or employment, provided it was done in contemplation or furtherance of a trade dispute.

The 'right' to strike

7.   Trade unions and the 'right' to strike were not, and are not, necessarily linked. The protection given by law to strikers (and formerly the penalties imposed by law) has not normally depended on whether they were union members or whether the strike was officially called by a union.

Savage penalties were exacted from striking workmen, as we have seen. The 1875 Act mitigated the criminal consequences of strike action, the 1906 Act mitigated the civil (tort) consequences. Although acts in furtherance of a trade dispute were protected, the protection did not extend to strikes for an ulterior, 'political' or non-industrial purpose. The landmark case of *Crofter Harris Tweed Co.* v. *Veitch*, [1942] A.C. 435, a decision of the House of Lords, cut down the scope of the exception by recognising that a combination to protect 'the promotion of the legitimate interests of the combiners' was not unlawful – what mattered was the 'predominant' or 'real' purpose of the combination.

8.   English law has never recognised a 'right to strike' as such. What it has done is to give ever-increasing immunities to those who resort to strike action. In this respect there is a sharp contrast with other laws, such as that of France, where the 'right to strike' is positively recognised by law.

The Industrial Relations Act 1971

9.   Critical writers (e.g. Kahn-Freund) treat this Act as 'a "strange interlude" in the evolution of our labour law'. But the Conservative government's attempt to regulate trade unions and industrial action by law (following the

14

initiative unsuccessfully launched by the preceding Labour government) is significant for two reasons: (1) It tried to extend legal control in the industrial sphere by distinguishing between lawful and unlawful strikes; (2) The return of a Labour government committed to reversing the effects of the Act not only meant a restoration of the *status quo ante*, but led to a further extension of trade union legal privileges and immunities.

10.   Two opposed views have been expressed about the Industrial Relations Act. One view sees the Act as demonstrating the folly of trying to regulate industrial relations and industrial action by law; the other view sees it as an attempt, albeit imperfect, to restore the balance between organised labour, the employers, and the consumers, and to reduce the 'No–Go Area' which modern industrial relations largely constitute. We do not choose between these views here; what is clear from the history of the Act is the difficulty that will be met in trying to solve the problems of industrial relations by the use of legal controls alone.

PART THREE

THE LEGAL BACKGROUND

In this Part we propose to discuss three matters briefly:
- A. The present legal position of trade unions in English law.
- B. The 'right to strike' in English law.
- C. Fundamental rights, freedom of association and the right to strike.

A. TRADE UNIONS IN ENGLISH LAW

Regulation of trade unions by law

1. The requirements of the 1971 Industrial Relations Act for the registration of trade unions have been repealed. Statutory requirements for modern trade unions are very few. A trade union may apply to the Certification Officer for 'listing', but requirements to satisfy the Certification Officer are few, and the consequences of listing are limited, other than its effects in setting the official seal on the listed union's independence. Unions must have written rules, but the law does not try to regulate what shall be contained in those rules. Members' rights against their union are very restricted; unions must conform to their rules in disciplinary matters, but the basis of discipline can be arbitrary or subjective, e.g., where rules give power to expel members for actions 'which are contrary to the interests of the union'.

All that the courts require is that trade unions should observe their own rules and the rules of natural justice in dealing with their members. But the protection given by these principles against arbitrary or oppressive action against individual members is slender and may be non-existent. Members who refuse to go on strike when directed

16

may thus render themselves liable to expulsion and hence, in an industry operating a closed shop, to loss of their jobs and perhaps of all hope of employment in their particular occupation, trade or profession.

2. Nor does the law control the way union officers or shop stewards are appointed, or the way decisions – e.g., to strike – are taken. 'The present law ... makes no attempt to guarantee union democracy' (*per* Sir Otto Kahn-Freund, who is broadly sympathetic to modern trade unions and their mode of operating). We shall not argue the issues for or against union democracy here, save to observe that they have tremendous significance in discussing strike action and its legitimacy. The decision to go on strike may be taken in a way which would be regarded as wholly undemocratic if applied to the management of a university or the conduct of any other sort of 'voluntary' organisation.

The legal privileges of unions

3. The protection given by the current legislation, re-enacting and extending the Trade Disputes Act 1906, means that trade unions (as well as individual strikers) are not liable for damages in tort for wrongs inflicted on others by their resort to strikes in contemplation or furtherance of a 'trade dispute'. The exact words of the Trade Union and Labour Relations Act 1974 (as amended), section 13, are worth quoting:

'An act done by a person in contemplation or furtherance of a trade dispute shall not be actionable in tort on the ground only (a) that it induces another person to break a contract or interferes or induces any other person to interfere with its performance; or (b) that it consists in his threatening that a contract (whether one to which he is a party or not) will be broken or its performance interfered

17

with, or that he will induce another person to break a contract or to interfere with its performance.'

'Trade dispute' is by the 1974 Act more broadly defined so as to include not only disputes between employers and workers but between workers and workers. Such disputes can be about individual contracts of employment or about the collective rights and recognition of bargaining groups (trade unions, facilities for shop stewards, and so on). An inter-union recognition battle is a trade dispute, and hence immune. A trade dispute need no longer be confined to Great Britain: there can be a trade dispute 'even though it relates to matters occurring outside Great Britain'; so a sympathetic British strike or boycott in support of a strike in the U.S. or Australia can be exempt.

4.   Section 14 of the T.U. & L.R.A. 1974 goes further in conferring on trade unions, their trustees, officials and members, a more general immunity from suits in tort, whether or not in furtherance of a trade dispute. The section provides in part:

'*Immunity of trade unions and employers' associations to actions in tort.*
(1) . . . no action in tort shall lie in respect of any act
(a) alleged to have been done by or on behalf of a trade union which is not a special register body . . .
(c) alleged to be threatened or to be intended to be done as mentioned in paragraph (a) or (b) above; against the union in its own name, or against the trustees of the union . . . or against any members or officials of the union . . . on behalf of themselves and all other members of the union'.

5.   Neither trade unions nor their members are licensed to commit crimes, or physical torts such as assault, or breaches

of contracts binding on them.* So malicious damage to company property, assaults on non-strikers and the like are still wrongs under civil law or criminal law. But economic injury to an employer, e.g., by damaging his business or losing him valuable contracts, is allowed by the trade union immunity.

6. Inducing a breach of contract by a trade union is immune from liability in tort. What about inducing a breach by 'intimidation'? *Rookes* v. *Barnard* [1964] A.C. 1129, a House of Lords decision, said that the wrong of intimidation could extend to inducing a breach of contract. Is this still good law? It seems not, by virtue of the Trade Disputes Act 1965 (= section 13(1) of the 1974 Act); but does this mean that there is no remedy if a breach of contract is induced by menaces? Presumably the menace of physical violence may still be prosecuted criminally, as will menaces corresponding to an 'unwarranted demand with menaces' (= blackmail) under the Theft Act; but a mere threat to turn away an employer's business, or to deter potential suppliers or customers, will not be actionable as intimidation.

7. Trade unions also remain liable for their contracts – with a vital exception. This is that practically every 'agreement' between a trade union and an employer – e.g., about manning levels, disputes procedures – is not legally enforceable unless specifically made so by the parties. Legally speaking such agreements are not worth the paper on which they are written, unless the terms of such an agreement are specifically incorporated in a contract between employer and employee.

---

* Though we cannot discuss the question in detail here, it should be remembered that in theory employees are liable to be sued for breach of their contracts of employment, as when they have taken part in wild-cat strikes or go-slows; but it would rarely if ever be worth the employer's while to do so.

19

The closed shop

8.   A further privilege accorded by the law is the recognition of closed shops, and the disallowance of the usual law of contract in that context. Whereas dismissal of an employee for trade union activity is specifically forbidden by law,* dismissal by an employer of an employee who refuses to join a union (or ceases to be a member of a union, e.g., because he was expelled) in a concern in which there is a 'union membership agreement' or closed shop, is specifically rendered lawful, and the unfair dismissals procedures do not apply to an employee dismissed for this reason.†

The Act does however provide that:

> 'An employee who genuinely objects on grounds of religious belief to being a member of a trade union shall have the right not to have action taken against him by his employer for the purpose of compelling him to belong to a trade union.'

This is the only exemption from compulsory membership of a closed shop apparently granted by English law.

Injunctions

9.   Lastly we note that not only are trade unions immune from actions for damages in respect of injuries inflicted in furtherance of a trade dispute, but also the private individual (and even the Attorney-General) will find it difficult to obtain an injunction from a court to restrain the trade union from inflicting such an injury.‡

10.   To sum up, trade unions now enjoy larger immunities

---

* Trade Union and Labour Relations Act, 1st Sched., para. 6(4).

† T.U. & L.R.A., 1st Sched., para. 6(5).

‡ See the case of *Gouriet* v. *Union of Post Office Workers* [1977] 3 All E.R. 70, where the House of Lords set out the position at length.

and privileges under English law than the Crown itself, which, since the Crown Proceedings Act 1947, has been amenable to civil suits for wrongs committed in its name. A question which needs discussion is whether this removal from the ambit of the law of a major and dominating force in British life (dominant outside the office and factory as well as in) should be continued.

The right to work in English law

11.   However, the English courts may not be entirely powerless, and a different approach has been revealed in some recent cases. The 'right to work' has received high judicial endorsement, and has been declared to be a fundamental principle of English law, breach of which would be against public policy and in restraint of trade.

We may start with *Nagle* v. *Feilden*.* The Court of Appeal had to consider the apparently arbitrary refusal by the Jockey Club of a trainer's licence to Mrs Nagle, on the ground only that she was a woman. It was argued that the Jockey Club had an unrestricted discretion whom to admit as a trainer. No, said Lord Denning. 'The common law of England has for centuries recognised that a man has a right to work at his trade or profession without being unjustly excluded from it. He is not to be shut out from it at the whim of those having the governance of it . . . . [To exclude a person on such a ground] is against public policy. The courts will not give effect to it.' The court ruled against the Jockey Club on this preliminary point.

12.   The same sort of point came up in the very recent 'Packer' case,† before Mr Justice Slade. Could the International Cricket Conference and the Test and County Cricket Board effectively prevent Packer players from playing in any Test or county match? Mr Justice Slade

* (1966) 1 All E.R. 689.
† *Greig* v. *Insole* [1978] 3 All E.R. 449.

decided that neither of these bodies was an employers' association, so that the point did not strictly arise for decision; but if these two bodies has been 'employers' assocations' within the Trade Unions and Labour Relations Act 1974, then they would have enjoyed the same sort of general immunity from actions in tort as a trade union. Employers, said the judge, might argue that they could agree that specified persons or categories of persons should be disqualified from seeking or remaining in employment with them; if this was challenged, the organisation might say that its rules, however unreasonable, could not be attacked as being in restraint of trade and it would enjoy general immunity from liability in tort. To this 'unattractive submission' there were two answers, said the learned judge, the second of which is very pertinent to our study of trade unions and their monopoly powers:

' . . . it is possible that, even if a hypothetical association formed for the purposes to which I have referred constituted an "employers' association" within the statutory definition, its rules could still be successfully attacked not so much on the grounds that they were in "restraint of trade", as on the broader grounds that they were contrary to public policy as preventing persons' right to work. A number of dicta of members of the Court of Appeal in *Nagle* v. *Feilden* suggest that, where an association exercises a virtual monopoly of human professional activity and seeks to exclude classes of men or women from such activity, the courts may intervene on broad grounds of public policy if the power is abused, without relying on the narrower doctrine of restraint of trade: see, for example, *per* Lord Denning, M.R., and *per* Danckwerts, L.J. As Danckwerts, L.J., said in that case – " . . . the courts have the right to protect the right of a person to work when it is being prevented by the dictatorial exercise of powers by a body which holds a monopoly".'

22

13.   Trade unions have, or may have, a monopoly of power, which they may feel they can exercise capriciously or arbitrarily. They may have power to make such rules as they please. But what is sauce for the employers' association goose can be sauce for the trade union gander as well. It will be interesting to see if English courts try to build on this prior, fundamental, common-law right to work so as to call in question some of the consequences of closed shops and boycotts of particular workers or classes of workers.

B.   THE 'RIGHT TO STRIKE' IN ENGLISH LAW

14.   This can shortly be dealt with by saying that in theory English law does not recognise the right to strike. A withdrawal of labour by an employee, whether acting alone or in concert with his fellows, is – if not in accordance with the terms of his contract – actionable by his employer as a breach of contract. In theory in each such case the employer may have the right to terminate the employee's contract for his fundamental breach of it.

15.   Although Lord Denning, Master of the Rolls, discussed the occasions when a strike 'would be perfectly lawful', in a case which was before the Court of Appeal in 1968,* in a recent speech at Birmingham University† he emphatically stated the opposite proposition:

'People sometimes spoke of a right to strike as if it were one of the fundamental rights of mankind. I would declare at once that there is no such right known to the law, not at any rate when it is used so as to inflict great harm on innocent bystanders, to disrupt essential services or to bring the country to a halt.

   So far as the law is concerned, those who do such things

* In *Morgan* v. *Fry* [1938] 3 All E.R. 452.
† Reported in *The Times*, 4 March 1978.

23

are exercising not a right but a great power, the power to strike.'

The better opinion is that there is no such right, but that the law, and industrial relations practice generally, tacitly recognise the distinction between an individual's failure to perform his contract and/or his termination of his employment on the one hand, and his temporary suspension of labour under a 'strike' on the other.

16. Go-slows and work-to-rules are also, or may be, breaches of the contract of employment. The employee is employed to do his job properly; and the courts today are not prepared to accept the excuse that by the work-to-rule employees were merely carrying out the employer's rules to the letter, and hence performing the contract faithfully. If their purpose, and the effect of their action, is to frustrate the business of their employer, then their action may be held in breach of their contracts, and hence unlawful.*

17. One must look, not only at the position of rank-and-file union members, but also at that of those who lead strikes – full-time union officials, shop stewards. These latter are granted complete immunity, irrespective of the basic breach of contract committed by the striking workers, provided only that they act in contemplation or furtherance of a trade dispute. Employees may be in breach of their individual contracts of employment by striking without due notice; other industrial action, such as go-slows and work-to-rules, cannot be legalised even if notice is given.

Picketing

18. Is there a right to picket? If so, what may be done by way of picketing? There seems to be considerable con-

* *Secretary of State for Employment* v. *ASLEF* (*No. 2*) [1972] 2 Q.B. 455 in the Court of Appeal.

fusion and uncertainty on both these questions, and such limited rights to picket as are accorded by the law are often abused or disregarded, as recent events have shown. In principle there is no right to picket, the only exceptions being those created by the Conspiracy and Protection of Property Act 1875. To be legal, picketing must satisfy the following conditions:

(i) It must be peaceful. Picketing which threatens or causes a breach of the peace or which is carried on by intimidation, assault, damage to property or violence will be a criminal offence.
(ii) Its sole legal purpose must be to communicate information and to persuade peacefully. Pickets have no right to stop persons, vehicles or goods, or to blockade premises. Pickets have no right to cause an obstruction by interrupting passage over a highway; if they do so, then they may have committed both criminal and civil wrongs.
(iii) It is illegal to follow persons about, so that the practice recently alleged of pickets chasing lorries up the motorway in cars was probably illegal. Pickets are not allowed to watch or beset premises, or picket the private homes of anyone, or commit theft of or damage to tools or equipment. Slashing of vehicle tyres (another practice recently alleged) would thus be an offence.
(iv) Picketing is not legal if it is not 'in contemplation or furtherance of a trade dispute'. This is a most important requirement, as it means that so-called 'secondary picketing' of firms not directly concerned with a dispute may be illegal.

19.   To summarise, picketing in breach of these requirements may be a criminal offence; but this law has been rarely enforced. The law is more concerned to regulate *methods* of picketing, while leaving the objects of picketing

almost entirely unregulated (except for the broad requirement set out at (iv) above).

Illegal strikes

20.   Persons following certain occupations (e.g., seamen at sea, police, post office workers, armed forces) are forbidden to strike by statute; but the list of these is short compared with the position in some other countries.

Some strikes may be illegal because of their consequences. It is a crime to break a contract of employment (e.g., by a strike or lockout without notice) where the consequences of such precipitate action are likely to endanger human life, cause serious bodily injury, or risk destruction or damage of valuable property: C. &. P.P.A. 1875 section 5 – but this law is rarely, if ever, invoked.

Under the Emergency Powers Act 1964 a government can take action to break strikes; and in time of war strikes may be rendered illegal by emergency legislation.

C.   FUNDAMENTAL RIGHTS, FREEDOM OF ASSOCIATION, AND THE RIGHT TO STRIKE

21.   'Freedom of association' appears in most of the international codes of human rights, notably in the Universal Declaration of Human Rights and in the European Convention on Human Rights. The 'right to strike' is, however, not expressly covered in either of these documents (though it is covered in the European Social Charter and in the International Covenant on Economic, Social, and Cultural Rights).

22.   We may start off with the *Universal Declaration of Human Rights*, made by the United Nations in 1948. This, by Article 23, provided that:

> '1. Everyone has the right to work, to free choice of employment, to just and favourable conditions of work

and to protection against unemployment . . .
3. Everyone who works has the right to just and favour-
able remuneration . . .
4. Everyone has the right to form and to join trade unions
for the protection of his interests.'

Article 20 deals with freedom of association:

'1. Everyone has the right to freedom of peaceful assembly
and association.
2. No one may be compelled to belong to an association.'

23. *The European Convention on Human Rights 1950* was
intended so far as the European countries parties to it were
concerned, 'to take the first steps for the collective enforcement of certain of the Rights stated in the Universal
Declaration'.
Article 11 of the Convention resembles the Universal
Declaration:

'1. Everyone has the right to freedom of peaceful assembly
and to freedom of association with others, including
the right to form and to join trade unions for the
protection of his interests.
2. No restrictions shall be placed on the exercise of these
rights other than such as are prescribed by law and are
necessary in a democratic society in the interests of
national security or public safety, for the prevention of
disorder or crime. or for the protection of health or
morals and for the protection of the rights and freedoms of others. This Article shall not prevent the
imposition of lawful restrictions on the exercise of
these rights by members of the armed forces, of the
police or of the administration of the State.'

According to Article 11, the freedom of association
includes the right to form and join. But it does not follow

Article 20(2) of the Universal Declaration by expressly prohibiting the 'closed shop' system.

Francis Jacobs, in his book on *The European Convention on Human Rights*, 1975, explains that, while freedom of association includes the right to form and join trade unions, it does not

> 'include the freedom *not* to join an association. Thus, Article 11 does not prohibit the "closed shop" system . . .' (p.157),

and he goes on to comment by way of historical explanation, that

> ' . . . on account of the difficulties raised by the "closed shop" system, it was considered undesirable to include the principles set out in Article 20(2) of the Universal Declaration of Human Rights, that no one may be compelled to belong to an association.'

(This point is also made by J. E. S. Fawcett in his book *The Application of the European Convention on Human Rights*, 1969, at p.223.)

24. *The European Social Charter* 1961, to which the United Kingdom is also a party, was designed to take the European Convention further in regard to 'social rights', which mainly refer to conditions of work.

By Part I the Contracting Parties accept as the aim of their policy, to be pursued by all appropriate means, both national and international in character, the attainment of conditions in which the following rights and principles may be effectively realised (among others):

> '(1) Everyone shall have the opportunity to earn his living in an occupation freely entered upon.
> (2) All workers have the right to just conditions of work.

28

(5) All workers have the right to freedom of association in national or international organizations for the protection of their economic and social interests.
(6) All workers and employers have the right to bargain collectively . . . .'

By Part II more detailed provision is made to carry out these principles, and the Contracting Parties declare themselves bound by the obligations undertaken under this Part. Article 1 deals with 'The Right to Work', and says in part:

'With a view to ensuring the effective exercise of the right to work, the Contracting Parties undertake:
(2) to protect effectively the right of the worker to earn his living in an occupation freely entered upon . . . .'

Article 2 spells out in detail the obligations under 'The Right to Just Conditions of Work'; and Articles 3, 4, 5, and 6 deal similarly with 'The Right to Safe and Healthy Working Conditions', 'The Right to a Fair Remuneration', 'The Right to Organise', and 'The Right to Bargain Collectively'. Article 6(4) recognises

'the right of workers and employees to collective action in cases of conflicts of interest, *including the right to strike*, subject to obligations that might arise out of collective agreements previously entered into.'
[Our italics]

The provisions of Article 6(4) are to be read in conjunction with the qualifications set out in the Appendix to the Social Charter, which says:

'It is understood that each Contracting Party may, insofar as it is concerned, regulate the exercise of the right to strike by law, provided that any further restriction that

29

this might place on the right can be justified under the terms of Article 31.'

And Article 31 in its turn provides that:

'1. The rights and principles set forth in Part I when effectively realised, and their effective exercise as provided for in Part II, shall not be subject to any restrictions or limitations not specified in those Parts, *except such as are prescribed by law and are necessary in a democratic society for the protection of the rights and freedoms of others or for the protection of public interest, national security, public health, or morals.*

2. The restrictions permitted under this Charter to the rights and obligations set forth herein shall not be applied for any purpose other than that for which they have been prescribed.'
[Our italics]

25.   Reference should also be made to the two International Labour Organisation Conventions – of 1948, concerning freedom of association and protection of the rights to organise; and of 1949, concerning the application of the principles of the right to organise and to bargain collectively, which have been ratified by the United Kingdom.

26.   *The International Covenant on Economic, Social, and Cultural Rights* 1966 of the United Nations was designed to amplify the corresponding provisions of the Universal Declaration. It came into force in 1976 after having received the necessary number of ratifications, including that of the United Kingdom. It is exceptional in mentioning the right to strike in Article 8:

'1. The States Parties to the present Covenant undertake to ensure:
(a)   The right of everyone to form trade unions *and join the union of his choice.*

30

(c) The right of trade unions to function freely subject to no limitations other than those prescribed by law and which are necessary in a democratic society in the interests of national security or public order *or for the protection of the rights and freedoms of others.*

(d) *The right to strike, provided that it is exercised in conformity with the laws of the particular country.'*
[Our italics]

Applicability of these provisions in the United Kingdom

27.   The Universal Declaration of Human Rights was adopted, without a single negative vote, by the General Assembly of the United Nations in 1948, but it provides no enforcement machinery either within each State or at a supranational level; nor will its terms prevail against the national law of a State. Its object was to set a standard of civilised behaviour by States; its terms state general principles applicable to all peoples and nations and would thus be relevant in international political controversies.

The United Kingdom is a party to the European Convention on Human Rights and is thus in international law bound by its provisions and is amenable to the jurisdiction of the European Commission and Court of Human Rights. The United Kingdom has also accepted the right of individual petition to the Commission in cases of alleged breach of the Convention, or the supplementary Protocols to which it is a party, and has made a declaration recognising the jurisdiction of the European Court of Human Rights. Although the provisions of the Convention do not as yet form part of the internal law of the United Kingdom, the Convention has ultimate legal force in that a person aggrieved by denial of any right protected by the Convention can invoke the machinery of the Commission set up by the Convention.

The position is similar in regard to the application of the International Covenant on Economic, etc., Rights in the United Kingdom, save that there is no provision in the Covenant for adjudication on alleged breaches of the Covenant.

28. So much, then, for the detailed provisions of the various international agreements for the protection of fundamental human rights, in the context of the right to strike. As we have seen, these provisions relate particularly to the 'freedom of association', and to other freedoms. What are the practical implications of this sort of provision? There is a powerful case for saying that, in this sort of context, 'freedom', if it has any meaning, means not merely the freedom to choose to do something, but also the freedom to choose not to do it. A one-way freedom is a logical contradiction. 'Freedom of association', so far as it relates to the formation and membership of trade unions of workers, must imply a freedom not to associate, i.e., a freedom not to belong; and the West German Constitutional Court has indeed ruled that the constitutional right to freedom of association necessarily implies the freedom not to associate.

Arguments used against this latter aspect of freedom, and supporting the right to set up closed shops and debar non-members of approved unions from employment, seem difficult to support. *Pace* Kahn-Freund, there is no essential similarity between the right to vote and the right to belong to a trade union. Failure to vote, except in some dictatorial States, is not penalised with loss of employment. The analogy is apt only to the extent that the non-joiner cannot be heard to complain of trade union decisions and conduct if he refuses to join, just as the non-voter cannot complain about government decisions if he opts out of the political process.

If one accepts the last point, this does not mean that

trade unions, any more than States, can do whatever they like – introduce oppressive or immoral legislation, say, in the case of governments; conduct their affairs undemocratically or use concerted strike action immorally in the case of unions. An immoral act voted by the majority cannot bind the minority who belong, still less those who do not.

The countervailing freedoms of the individual, set beside the collective freedoms of unions and governments, are all-important. These freedoms include: the right not to be coerced; the right not to be punished except for a crime whose terms and penalties are declared by law; the right that those who take decisions in their name should be genuinely responsive to the wishes, views, and interests of those they rule.

PART FOUR

WHEN IS IT RIGHT TO STRIKE?

A. THE MORAL ISSUES AND CHOICES

If it's legal, it's OK

1. We can immediately dispose of two arguments or justifications which are often resorted to if a particular strike is criticised as unjustifiable or wrong. The first is:

'If it's legal, it's OK!'

In other words, there is nothing in the law which says we must not strike on this particular occasion, or use this particular form of industrial action, however damaging it may be to others; so there is nothing wrong in going ahead.

2. There are two answers to this:

(a) The law in Britain has largely opted out of industrial relations, at least so far as industrial disputes and action are concerned: trade unions have immunity from civil proceedings in regard to acts done in furtherance of a trade dispute, such as inducing workers to break their contracts. So it is the rule, rather than the exception, for strike action to be unregulated by law. What the law says cannot, therefore, be a criterion of the rightness or wrongness of industrial action.

(b) Anyhow, a man's moral duty goes much further than abstaining from illegal acts. Morality may command one not to do what one has a legal power or right to do. An example would be where to expose the quite true facts about another person's social or moral delinquencies in youth may not be prohibited by the law of defamation, and yet it could be a grossly uncharitable and hence immoral act to reveal them. The law itself recognises that legal rights must not be

34

abused. The concept of 'abuse of rights' is a well-known one in foreign legal systems; but in English law too the doctrine of public policy, the rules of 'equity', and judicial control of the exercise of administrative discretions by public authorities, are all examples where a person with a particular legal right or power will be prevented from exercising it for an unjust purpose, or with a grossly unfair result.

The morality of an act is partly defined by its consequences; bankruptcy for an employer, loss of employment by fellow-workers, grave injury to third parties unconnected with a dispute, may all be consequences of the legal act of withdrawing one's labour, and may render unjust what is otherwise justifiable. Life in society would be intolerable if everyone took what the law permits as their only guide to their personal behaviour.

We have no alternative
3. The argument often used is:
    'We have no alternative'
– meaning that if we want to pursue our wage claim, enforce a closed shop, compel management to a certain course of action, oblige government to do something, force consumers to bring *their* pressure to bear on those who can give us what we want, then it is *not merely legitimate* for us to resort to strike action which would otherwise offend against the norms set out in this Part, *it is essential* for us to take that action.

That argument too is a false one. It appears valid on the surface because the unspoken assumption of a conditional sentence has been suppressed. The full sentence should read:
    '[If we want to succeed in our claim or objective, and all morally legitimate ways of persuading those with

35

power to give us what we want would fail, then] we have no alternative [but to use morally illegitimate means].'

Every man with free will always has some alternative, though it may indeed on occasion be an unpalatable one. Morality, however, cannot be seen simply as the satisfaction of one's wants, if only because people's wants on occasions conflict. In these cases, regard has to be had for considerations of justice, and the morally defensible alternative may require us to disregard our own wants to some extent.

4. There are cases where legitimate and moderate requests or demands have not been met, where gross injustice continues in our conditions of employment, and where other means of remedying these injustices may have become legitimated thereby, even if harm is incidentally inflicted on the innocent non-participant. But even here we retain the alternative, the choice; maybe we have to submit to injustice rather than create greater injustice. Maybe we must seek a remedy in ways other than industrial action. In every case we must still weigh the consequences, and we cannot act unless the moral balance is decisively tilted in our favour.

If we go ahead when the moral balance is against us, because we have the power to do so, we must remember that *power does not legitimate itself*. Having the legal or economic power to do something does not alone give us any moral entitlement to do it.

The basis of moral choice

5. Law, power, necessity are not sufficient justifications for industrial action. The justice of our demand may be outweighed by the injustice that our action will inflict upon others. If we are to make a moral choice, to what principles should we look for guidance?

36

The gospels and epistles, to which one would be tempted to look for an answer, seem not to provide one in sufficient detail to help us in the particular case we are confronted with. There is no primer of industrial relations to be found in the New Testament. Scattered texts, such as 'The labourer is worthy of his hire' (Luke 10, 7), while true, are not sufficient – of what hire is the labourer worthy, and what may he do if he does not get it? St John the Baptist, while appearing to advocate the welfare state and equalisation of resources on the one hand:

'He who has two coats, let him share with him who has none; and he who has food, let him do likewise . . .'

immediately afterwards tells the soldiers who ask what they should do:

'Rob no one by violence or by false accusation, and be content with your wages.' (Luke 3, 10–14),

which seems a recipe for a wage freeze.

6. But our mistake is an elementary one: industrial relations are not a department of life set apart from the world of morality and neighbourliness – they are an integral part of it. We must behave as morally when we get to work as when we return home. And the gospels and epistles *do* contain a primer of *human* relations. It is unnecessary to spell out all the teaching which tells us how to conduct our lives in society in accordance with God's plan. It suffices to recall the great second commandment, 'Love your neighbour as yourself'; which being interpreted means that we must be as active in looking after our brother's welfare as our own. Our claims and our interests are not paramount. And our brothers, those whom we should so regard, are not just our family and workmates, important though they are; our managers, our customers, our patients, our own employees, are also our brothers. The confrontational and self-regarding style of modern industrial relations, which denies the human claims of

anyone to be a brother who is not a fellow-employee, is contrary to the gospels.*

The first sin in industrial relations is thus confrontation based on exclusion, on denial of brotherhood. The second is selfishness. The third sin is that of employers who exploit their work-force – who defraud their workers of their due reward.

The right to work

7. Everyone has the right to work, to engage in productive activity, to maintain himself and those for whom he is responsible. Denial of this right is a denial of a fundamental human right. It is much more difficult, however, to determine just what claims can be supported by appeal to this right. A full-scale treatment of the moral basis and scope of the right to work is beyond our present task, but perhaps an attempt to clarify it in an informal way can be made. The right to work does not mean that everyone must be permitted to undertake, still less to be paid for, any work he chooses. Economic demand and facilities, the skills necessary for entering a trade or profession, statutory regulation of employment, are all perfectly legitimate constraints on the individual's free choice of work.

8. What about union membership? Is a legal restriction,

*See the judgment of Lord Atkin in *Donoghue* v. *Stevenson*, [1932] A.C. 562, which introduced the 'Good Neighbour' principle embodied in the parable of the Good Samaritan into English law. Lord Atkin put it this way, in words which have been frequently quoted since: 'You must take reasonable care to avoid acts or omissions which you can reasonably foresee would be likely to injure your neighbour. Who, then, in law is my neighbour? The answer seems to be – persons who are so closely and directly affected by my act that I ought reasonably to have them in contemplation as being so affected when I am directing my mind to the acts or omissions which are called in question'. And see also the statement of the Commission for International Justice and Peace of the English Hierarchy in 1977, which stressed that the modern company must be seen as a partnership involving management, employees, customers, and the public at large which is affected by its operations.

or a social restriction imposed by a trade union or work-force through resort to the strike weapon, justifiable if it prevents persons who do not belong to the appropriate union from being engaged or retained in employment?

We do not propose to discuss the morality of the *closed shop* here. There are arguments advanced both for it and against it on moral grounds. But since it is maintained in being by the threat of industrial action, the moral quality of the strike to obtain or to maintain a closed shop must be judged by the individual worker who is faced with this problem in the light of the general principles set out in this Statement.

9. (a) If a closed shop is immoral, or operated immorally, so as to contradict a fundamental right to work, then use of the strike to establish or support it must in its turn be immoral and unjustifiable.

    (b) If a closed shop is neutral, in itself neither good nor bad, then the morality of strike action to obtain or maintain it must be judged objectively according to the criteria we set out below.

    (c) If a closed shop is desirable, not only permissible but actively to be encouraged in particular trades, industries or professions, it is still not permitted to use immoral means to obtain a moral end. In judging the moral quality of the means, we must have regard to the overall effect of one's actions, the decisive balance of moral advantage, as determined by these same criteria.

The right not to work

10. There are many societies around the world where work is a legal duty imposed by the State, and failure to work may be a criminal offence punishable as parasitism. (The Soviet Union springs to mind in this connexion.) This was the attitude in England under the Poor Law. Sturdy

rogues and vagabonds without visible means of support were liable to penalties.

11.   In modern Britain it is no longer a criminal offence not to work. The work-shy are in practice often able to rely on social security for their needs; and even if not they, then their dependants, for whom they should provide, may be provided for by the State.* Children, the old, the sick, the unfortunate, are already looked after if they do not or cannot work. But we must deal here with a different problem, where the employee refuses to perform the work he has agreed to do under his contract of employment. Not every such refusal is a strike, by any means; laziness and incompetence may also come in. There are two situations which we must look at:

    (a) The employee resigns his employment.

    (b) The employee 'goes on strike'.

12.   If an employee resigns his employment, one may think that that is his individual affair. He may be liable civilly for damages for breach of contract, but that is all (and usually it is not worth the employer's while to pursue even this remedy). The employee does not expect or demand re-engagement. No court will compel him by specific performance to do what he refuses to do. To hold otherwise would be to enforce slavery. We may therefore say that, whatever the legal position, the employee may effectively terminate his employment at any time.

To do so may in some circumstances be immoral. On the fact of his having engaged the employee to do a particular job, the employer may have entered into onerous and

---

* 'Where a person persistently refuses or neglects to maintain himself or any person whom he is liable to maintain . . . ', and in consequence of his refusal or neglect housing accommodation has to be provided for him or any other person by a local authority, or supplementary benefit or free board and lodging in a reception centre has to be provided for him or some other person for whose maintenance he is responsible, then a criminal offence is committed: National Assistance Act 1968, s.51, and Supplementary Benefits Act 1976, s.25.

costly commitments. Other persons may be relying on the employer to supply what it is his business to supply, and may suffer damage if this is not supplied when wanted, due to the employee's default.

But one can think of examples where the voluntary resignation of an employee produces an effect similar to that of a strike, and where similar grave moral considerations apply. For instance, all the doctors in government employment in a particular area may simultaneously tender their resignations in order to force their demands on their employer. Exactly this happened with the doctors' 'strike' in Nigeria. The catastrophic result is the total removal of health care from the affected area.

13. Where an employee 'goes on strike', he ceases to do the work for which he was engaged, but he does not intend to terminate his employment (though the common law may say that that is the effect of his breach of contract). The employee does not expect to get paid while he is on strike; but he expects that, after a period of contention, in which he hopes to get what he wants, he will be taken on the work-force again as if nothing had happened. The state of 'being on strike' is thus an anomalous one.

The right not to be injured

14. Everyone has the right not to be injured by the intentional or careless acts of others. This is as fundamental a right, fundamental to any legal system* as to any system of morality, as the right to work or the right to withhold one's labour.

Innocent third parties who are not directly concerned with a dispute have a greater right than those who by their relationship and their behaviour in that relationship have accepted or provoked action which may harm them.

* This right was strongly re-affirmed in *Donoghue* v. *Stevenson*.

41

B. THE FACTORS WHICH DETERMINE OUR CHOICE

15.   In order to weigh up the morality of our choice to strike/take industrial action or not, and the type of action to take, we must assess the various factors involved. These factors comprise:

- – the form of action taken;
- – the purpose of the action;
- – the relationships involved; i.e., between the takers of industrial action and persons affected by the action;
- – the consequences; i.e., the effects which the action will have.

I. The action: the MEANS

The action taken includes:

- (i) the *processes* by which the decision to act is taken;
- (ii) the *choices* of action open.

Processes

16.   One particular means of deciding to strike, e.g., by show of hands, is not necessarily inferior to another, e.g., by secret ballot; but all means of decision which tend to lead to *intimidation* or to *opting out* of the moral choice are morally inferior, and may even be wrong.

17.   Proceeding without negotiation or consultation, whether or not laid down in a procedure agreement, may be immoral, because unfair; and when the action taken is grave, e.g., an immediate decision to strike, it may be seriously wrong. Breach of an agreement is itself a breach of faith; but – unless one's wish is to do damage to an antagonist, rightly or wrongly – one should remember that precipitate action without forewarning is likely to damage his interests and make an amicable solution less likely.

The form of industrial action
18. On the part of employees this includes: mass with-drawal of labour ('strike'); go-slow (performing con-tracted work inadequately or incompletely; union meet-ings in company time at times inconvenient for the production process, etc.); boycotts and blacking, etc. On the part of employers industrial action includes especially mass dismissals ('lockouts').

19. An immoral form of industrial action cannot be justified by its end or motive. For example, it will be difficult to justify industrial sabotage or the deliberate infliction, by physical violence or otherwise, of pain and suffering on the target person(s), whatever the end of motive in sight.

20. *The degree of industrial action* must be the *MINI-MUM* necessary to achieve the end, provided (a) the end, and (b) the means, are in themselves morally justifiable.
   The reason for this principle of minimalism is that by definition industrial action must inflict some harm on some other person or body (the 'target'). Infliction of harm may be completely unjustified, because either the target is an inappropriate one, or the degree of harm cannot be justified by the degree of injustice complained of by the persons taking industrial action. Even where there is justification, one must inflict as little harm as possible. Thus a mass walkout over a trivial grievance, or a go-slow which gravely harms third parties, cannot be justified, in the former case because there is no proportionality be-tween complaint and action taken, and in the latter case because the harm is not inflicted on the author of the injustice, if any.

21. To resort to a strike should be the ultimate step, not

the first one, in the settling of a dispute.* Strikes, as explained in para. 13, are the withdrawal of labour, entailing the loss of pay. Not doing one's job (e.g., by various forms of go-slow or boycott), but getting the pay for the job, can rarely be justified. Not to do what one is paid to do is taking what one has not earned. Many forms of industrial action may thus be wrong in themselves.

22. The individual cannot justify his resort to industrial action by saying that it was not his decision, but the decision of his union leaders/shop stewards/workmates. It is always his decision. But the desire for solidarity often leads employees to co-operate with a decision to strike which they do not personally agree with. Solidarity with one's workmates is not a bad thing, and in the past has been a most important source of strength in overcoming injustice. But at best solidarity can only go to *excuse* or *explain*, it cannot go to *justify*, an immoral strike.

23. Depriving employees of their livelihood, industrial action by an employer, is a catastrophic act which can rarely be justified, except for clear and fundamental breaches of the basis upon which the contract of employment is founded.

II. The purpose of the action: the END or MOTIVE
What is the hoped-for end or the motive for the action?
24. From the employees' side, the end may be:

Pay and conditions
(a) to remedy injustices in their employment from which they suffer (*remedy personal injustice*); or

---

* See *Gaudium et Spes* (CTS Do 363), n.68: 'In the event of economic-social disputes all should strive to arrive at peaceful settlements. The first step is to engage in sincere discussion between all sides; but the strike remains even in the circumstances of today a necessary (although an ultimate) means for the defence of workers' rights and the satisfaction of their lawful aspirations.'

(b) to remedy injustices in their employment from which their fellow workers in that employment suffer (*altruistic*); or

(c) to obtain better pay or conditions (*personal betterment*).

Structural goals

(d) to change the structures in which they work e.g., to obtain participation in decision-making (*structural change*); or

(e) to procure the employment or dismissal of particular employees or supervisors, e.g., an unpopular foreman, coloured workers (*eliminate individual employees*); or

(f) to pursue some goal set by the unions or worker-representatives in regard to union organisation, discipline or control, e.g., to impose a closed shop, obtain bargaining recognition (*union position and functions*).

External goals

(g) to support action by workers in other industries or employments, e.g., by sympathetic strike, boycott (*altruistic external goals*); or

(h) to obtain some non-employment objective, e.g., to ban trade with a foreign country, prevent building of nuclear power stations (*political objectives*).

25. In the scale in which the justification for industrial action is weighed, (a) and (b) remedy substantial injustice, such as low pay or exploitative conditions, and will weigh heavily. (c). The desire to share in the profits of a successful company, to ameliorate one's lot, is not unworthy; and justice may demand that the employers/shareholders/customers should give a due proportion of any increase in wealth to workers who have earned it by their labours. But mere desire for greater wealth or less work cannot act as a justification for acts with harmful consequences – the greater the harm, whether to the employer or to third

parties (customers, the users of services or goods), the less justifiable the action.

26. (d). The moral weight to be attached to the demand for structural change depends on one's evaluation of the moral desirability of what is sought. Workers' participation in controlling their own destinies and work may have a high value; it may be considered a recognition of human values which should be present in every work-place – *or* it may be unjustifiable in that type of work. Industrial action in pursuit of the former may well be justified if other means of pressing the point fail.

27. (e). Going on strike to get rid of an unpopular employee may be a morally justifiable act, where the employee abuses his power, sabotages the work of his fellows, and so on – *or* it may be one of the greatest evils, when pressure is brought to bear to get rid of one who does his duty conscientiously and fairly, e.g., to detect thieving, or as a foreman to stop workers skiving, or to perform his own work effectively.

28. (f). Belonging to a union does not exempt one from moral responsibility. Action taken by a union is not outside the moral sphere. To seek to obtain advantages for unions may be a legitimate end; but it is not so if it seeks to inflict disproportionate harm on individuals or groups. We do not evaluate the morality of the closed shop here – but the question can be posed, 'Is it wrong to deprive others of their "right to work"?' If a closed shop in general or in the particular case is immoral, strike action in support of it is wrong too (see paras. 8 to 9 above).

In any case, union ends (f), as they are less close to the remedying of personal injustices (a), or even the obtaining of personal betterment (c), weigh *less heavily* in the scale; they can justify only a lesser degree of harm to the target, and even less to any third party.

29. (g). The same is true of external goals. If we should

not inflict disproportionate harm on innocent third parties in remedying personal injustice, how much the less are we entitled, in pursuit of a grievance which is not ours, to harm innocent persons or classes of persons who are not parties to the dispute at all, and against whom we have no grievance?

III. The nature of the relationships involved

30. The relationships involved are:

(a) between the parties in dispute;

(b) with others (third parties) affected by their action.

Why it is vital to define who are parties to a dispute is because harm which may be legitimately inflicted against a party to a dispute *if the cause is just* (see II), ceases to be legitimate if inflicted against non-parties (see IV).

(a) Parties in dispute

31. That is, the persons striking or taking industrial action and those with whom they are in a contractual relationship. Usually this means the employer. Sometimes, where the immediate employer is a subsidiary, or wholly controlled or paid for by another, that other is also an indirect party in the dispute. Thus a strike against a subsidiary may be directed against a parent company; a strike against a public department or corporation may be directed against the government which subsidises or controls it. (Tax-payers, rate-payers, or consumers at large are not parties to a dispute involving a corporation which their rates and taxes, or their purchases, support.)

32. Where the dispute is not 'really' between immediate employer and employee, because it is against a particular employee or employees, or is for some external goal, like a sympathetic strike, the immediate employer is in truth not a 'party in dispute', but an innocent third party; and the

harm inflicted on an innocent third party requires much greater justification.

(b) Third parties not in dispute

33. Apart, then, from employers who are not the real targets of a sympathetic strike, these are all those who are not in a contractual relationship with the persons taking industrial action, such as:

- passengers affected by an air-controllers' go-slow;
- patients in hospital (or not admitted to hospital) affected by a strike in the Health Service;
- house-owners in a firemen's strike;
- trade customers of a company in dispute;
- school-children affected by teachers' work-to-rule;
- importers affected by a dock strike;
- practically everyone affected by a miners' strike or electricity workers' strike.

34. The tendency is for the innocent to suffer increasingly from industrial disputes to which they are not parties, and whose outcome, save by suffering or by public protests, they cannot affect. Despite disclaimers, suffering by these *indirect targets* (the direct target being the legal employer) is often an essential ingredient of the strikers' strategy. If the indirect targets suffered no harm, the strikers would lose a major part of their leverage. This does *not* mean that the strikers are therefore justified in using this leverage.

35. The relationships involved can be analysed in a different way:

(i) Relationships concerned with the *supply of an essential service or good*, essential *either because it is vital to life and well-being* – care of the sick, water, electricity; *or* because the supplier is a *monopoly*, lack of whose service or goods would gravely damage a particular trade, industry, or activity – oxygen, railways, post.

(ii) Relationships which do not affect essential services or supplies.

36. The division between (i) and (ii) is not the same as that between public and private enterprises (though often essential services are provided by public bodies). Thus there are private hospitals; petrol is supplied by private corporations, as is oxygen. So one cannot make a moral rule which distinguishes public from private services – the fundamental difference is between essential and non-essential goods and services.

37. However, what is non-essential for the public at large may be essential for a particular user. A small company which cannot get a particular raw material vital to its manufacturing process may be forced out of business, and its workers forced out of employment – it may be affected, even if not an indirect target of industrial action, as an innocent third party.

IV. The effects of the industrial action on the parties to the dispute, and on third parties

Responsibility

38. If a man wills an act, he wills also the consequences which he can or should foresee as probably resulting from that act. This is a rule of morality as well as of law. English law, with its notion of *mens rea* or guilty mind, took over from Christian morality the idea that a sane person is legally responsible for harm which he intended to inflict or which he could foresee or could reasonably be expected to foresee would follow from his actions. It is no answer in law for someone who does something to say that he never thought about the consequences, if he should have thought about them; nor that the act he did was not intended to injure the person who has suffered harm; nor that the act he did was harmless in itself. He will still be liable.

It is the same with moral responsibility, except that responsibility in morality goes far wider than the responsibility which the law imposes. *We are morally obliged to think about the consequences of our acts; and we are answerable for harmful consequences which cannot be morally justified.*

39.   Industrial relations sometimes give the impression of being totally removed from the control of morality as well as from the control of law. Enormously harmful consequences are inflicted on the innocent in pursuit of an industrial end, without compunction or remorse. Hospital patients – to take a recent example – suffer discomfort, pain, and agony of mind, or may even die, because of 'industrial action'. Others suffering from grave illness cannot even gain admission to treatment.

The answer given by those who inflict this harm is that it is not their fault or responsibility, but the fault of those who deny them what they are seeking. They accept that there is a responsibility, but claim it is not theirs. This argument can too easily justify what one may term *industrial terrorism*; just like terrorists proper, who claim that it is the injustice of society, or the stubbornness of governments, which 'causes' them to blow up trains filled with innocent fellow-citizens.

Social responsibility
40.   Our society is interconnected and interrelated. The action or inaction of one sector of society readily affects many other sectors. This is the consequence of the modern industrial economy built on the division of labour. It is hard to imagine an industry, employment or activity so isolated from the rest of society that disturbance within it will not affect the rest of society in some way.

41.   Our interconnectedness means *interdependence*. We depend on each other, We do not grow our own food,

50

gather our own fuel, heal our own illnesses, make our own machines, teach our own children. Interdependence is one of the marks of the *civilised society*, by which we mean a society in which each member recognises his obligations to every other member. The dependence is mutual: we depend on the milkman for our milk; he depends on us for his transport, home, protection, food and for the education of his children.

42. Interdependence creates *social responsibility*. We cannot evade or avoid it, except by withdrawing from civilised society. We must assess the social consequences of our actions before we initiate them.

The remoter persons or groups are from the relationship and causes of an industrial dispute, the more difficult, morally speaking, it is to justify *indirect harm* inflicted on them as a consequence of that dispute. Where *direct harm*, i.e., directly willed harm, is inflicted on innocent third parties, and where the harm suffered is serious and not trivial, then it is almost impossible to conceive of a case where the action is not morally wrong. The greater the harm, the more innocent the sufferers, the wider the circle of suffering, the greater the evil.

43. It is not enough for the individual person not to *participate* in evil acts; he must not *acquiesce* in them or *condone* them. Rather must he *oppose* them, and try to create structures in which such acts will be impossible or strongly sanctioned or condemned. Pilate washed his hands; we cannot do that when faced with immoral industrial action.

C. QUESTIONS TO ASK AND ANSWER

44. These are questions which, on the basis of the principles just set out, every person who is required to choose whether to participate in industrial action or not, or to judge the morality of such an action, must ask himself:

Means

Q.1. Is the form of industrial action
  (a) appropriate and proportionate to the end in view?
  (b) the minimum that the situation requires, and which inflicts the minimum of harm?
  (c) not itself a wrong thing to do?

Q.2. Has the decision to take that action
  (a) been taken by a reasonable procedure?
  (b) been carefully considered by any individual taking or joining in the action, who accepts his personal moral responsibility for the act and its consequences, as they affect third parties as well as the immediate target of the action?

Purposes

Q.3. Is the purpose or aim of the industrial action
  (a) to remedy injustice suffered by those who act?
  (b) to remedy injustice suffered by fellow-workers in the same employment?
  (c) to obtain better pay and conditions?
  (d) to change the structures of employment?
  (e) to achieve an organisational aim of unions or labour representatives?
  (f) to support claims or action in other industries or concerns?
  (g) to achieve a political or non-industrial end?

Q.4. What is the moral weight of the purpose for which the industrial action is taken? (Bear in mind that the weight of such action is likely to be greater if the purpose comes high on the list given under Q.3, and less if the purpose comes lower down the list.)

Relationships

Q.5. Who are the parties to the dispute? Who are the

immediate, and who are the indirect, targets of the industrial action?

Q.6. Who, although not parties to the dispute, will be affected by the action?

Consequences

Q.7. (a) What are the consequences which will or may flow from the industrial action?

(b) Will they injure persons who are not parties to the dispute?

(c) Will they injure parties to the dispute to an unjustifiable degree?

(d) Will the consequence be to deprive persons of essential goods or services?

(e) How grave will the injury be that is caused by this deprivation?

(f) Will the industrial action transgress or deny a fundamental right of another person to life, liberty, health, freedom to work, or to family, religious or social relationships?

The moral decision

After carefully reviewing and answering the questions set out under Q.1 to Q.7 above, we should be in a position to answer the final question:

Q.8. Is the industrial action, bearing in mind its intrinsic quality, the appropriateness of its means, and its harmful consequences for parties and non-parties, morally justifiable?

To answer this, we must weigh in the balance the harms and benefits, the rights (of everyone) and the wrongs (of everyone). Only if the balance of moral advantage tilts decisively in the positive direction can we justify the industrial action in question. And this is just as true of

53

lockouts and action by employers as it is of strikes and action by employees.

D. OBJECTIONS AND REMEDIES

Objections
45. Two main objections may be brought by the worker who seeks conscientiously to answer the questions just posed, and who does not like the answer he may get, namely, that the industrial action mooted or started at his workplace is morally wrong and he ought not to participate in it, or even condone it.

The first objection is that by being forced by this catechism to rule out many forms of industrial action which are currently employed and tolerated, even if resented or feared (whether by those forced to take part in them, or by those injured by them), the result will be a form of '*industrial disarmament*'. 'Can one throw half one's weapons away?' someone may ask. 'Surely this means that we cannot fight for better pay as we have done in the past? Surely it means that workers in essential services may be debarred from initiating a strike which will be just? Surely all this is anti-union, and will impoverish the working class in the long run?'
46. Yes, a certain measure of industrial disarmament may follow. But if the weapons are evil, or the use of them morally wrong, will this be a bad thing? The parallel with warfare is apt. Morality cannot be suspended or abandoned while we fight a war, even a war of self-defence. The progressive move is to try to eliminate war, and the causes of war, and one step is to ban the use of weapons which inflict terrifying harm on the innocent. The positive aim is to create conditions of peace, and structures for the peaceful resolution of disputes. As in the international sphere, so in the industrial sphere: intensification of industrial

warfare, and the use of illegitimate weapons, must be wrong.

47.   But yes, one can continue to fight to remedy injustices, though in a spirit of brotherhood and not confrontation and attack. Industrial action may still be legitimate in these circumstances, as our catalogue of questions should show. Fighting for better pay may at some times be legitimate, and at other times simply a form of materialism and greed.

48.   Workers who provide essential services (and, because of the interdependence of society, the list of those who can menace the supply of essential services gets longer and longer) are at a moral disadvantage. It is up to society to remedy this by better structures. We look at this in paras. 53 to 61 below.

49.   If unions have become instruments for the infliction of injustice, or are so operated by their members or officials on occasion as to cause serious injustice, then it must be right and not wrong to be opposed to them, or to what they do. The remedy is to persuade union members and officials to act justly, and to devise structures which will help them so to act; see paras. 53 and 56 below.

50.   Materially *some* of the working class may be worse off if they cannot grab all that their muscle-power might enable them to take. This is true only of the minority of workers; most are impoverished more drastically by not being able to take part in the grabbing game. But if Christianity teaches us anything, it is that material wealth and possessions are not the only form of riches, and that eager pursuit of material wealth may in fact lead to something far worse, namely, *moral impoverishment*. To declare that morality has no part in ever-expanding circles of society and social life is to rob the society, and its members, of their moral integrity.

51.   The second objection is more profound, and touches

the heart more deeply. It is the anguished cry of the ordinary worker who in his heart agrees with all that is said here, but says: 'What can I, one lone individual faced with the mass meeting or the mass views of my workmates, do? I cannot stand out against my fellows. That would take moral courage which I do not have; and might harm my prospects of employment or even the welfare of my family.' One sympathises deeply: how often do worthy people remain silent when they should speak, tolerate injustice which they theoretically should not do! Anyone in a communist or totalitarian State knows all about the moral dilemma this poses.

52. Our answer to this *cri de coeur* is three-fold:

(i) You are not alone. For all you know, and you may well already know or suspect this, many, perhaps even the majority, think like you: how will this become apparent and change the way things are done if you remain silent?

(ii) It is up to those who devise the structures for deciding on industrial organisation, relations, and action to make sure that the ordinary person's voice can be fully heard, without fear and with its full effect. Structural remedies are called for: we must devise and implement them (see para. 54 below).

(iii) There comes a time when one must swim against the tide. Christianity is not a religion of conformism to the world's demands. Christ came to change the world, not confirm it in its selfish and immoral attitudes. The pressure to conform to the world's attitudes and behaviour today, whether it is in material things, sexual attitudes, or political ideas, is tremendous. The world will never change for the better if the individuals who compose it do not accept their moral responsibility to try to change it; and the beginning of that change is to work out our own moral position, to apply it in our daily life, and to make it known to those with whom we live and work – not in a spirit of dogma and confrontation, but in a spirit of loving concern and brotherhood.

Remedies

53. Those who have power over their fellow-citizens, whether they are politicians, teachers, trade union officials, employers or thinkers and writers, have a colossal responsibility to discharge. They cannot lecture others on their moral responsibility, or impose structures to enforce them, without accepting their own far larger moral responsibility to shape institutions and attitudes which will help ordinary citizens to achieve the goals set out above and to enjoy (for themselves and their families) the justice they are entitled to. Some possible remedies, whether to prevent injustice or to fill gaps left by the outlawing of some forms of industrial action, are discussed below. This, though, can only be a preliminary statement of possibilities; some may not be practicable or acceptable, while there may be others of which we have not thought.

54. The procedures for resolving industrial disputes need radical revision in many instances. It is not our task to try to legislate, or to advise legislation, for achieving this end; but there are certain essential criteria which must be met – management as well as labour, the public (through government and public opinion) as well as shareholders, have a joint responsibility for bringing about these changes. The first task is to improve the means of avoiding having to resort to industrial action. Radical steps include forms of industrial partnership, of worker-management or worker-participation in the capital of the enterprise; these are naturally only possible where there is a capital, and where worker-management does not mean that other essential interests, e.g., of customers, are neglected or over-

ridden. So this does not meet the case in public enterprises where a service or a benefit is provided, e.g., railways, electricity, hospitals, education, government administration; here other structural remedies are needed.

Less radical steps involve proper consultative machinery, where consultation is not done either out of fear or as a matter of mere form, but genuinely because workers in any kind of enterprise must be more than hired hands, however well paid. Procedures for consulting and resolving disputes before they arise are not enough by themselves; there must be a willingness to work them and to abide by them. One of the commonest stories these days is of unofficial and even official action which contravenes procedure agreements designed to eliminate disputes or enable their peaceful settlement. As we point out (see para. 17), the fact that an agreement is not legally binding does not in morality justify the breaking of that agreement.

55. The method by which the decision to strike or take industrial action is made needs scrutiny. If the decision to strike is a moral decision, as we say it is, then it must be taken in a conscientious way. It is hard to see how, in many cases, a mass decision by show of hands at a mass meeting can fairly permit the individual to decide for himself, and express his decision freely. (We exclude altogether consideration of allegations that on occasion there is trickery, manipulation, or intimidation in such votes – if this is so, then the decision in that instance is immorally taken, and cannot bind.) This principle argues for the adoption of secret ballots wherever possible, though we can imagine many legitimate cases – e.g., men in a particular machine shop – where it is possible to decide freely and without secret voting to take or not to take some form of action.

56. Consultation between unions and their members, and between shop-stewards and employees, is just as important

as between management and labour. An individual worker or trade union member must accept the moral responsibility for his own decision – which is often with grave consequences for others – to strike or to take industrial action. He cannot delegate that decision to others, e.g., the union or the shop stewards, and so escape moral responsibility. This implies that the unions and the stewards in their turn must respect the moral responsibilities of their members or fellow-workers, which they can do by fairly taking their opinions before recommending or enforcing industrial action of any kind.

We are disturbed to find that many employees seem to be in fear of their union representatives or shop stewards; and that they tend to class the unions as 'they' along with their employers – 'they insist that we do such and such'; instead of feeling that the union is them and speaks for them. If this is so, the remedy is not in our hands; but the extension and improvement of proper consultative machinery between unions and their members would go far to alleviate this.

57. So far as essential services are concerned, the steady deterioration in moral standards and in perception of social responsibility must be reversed. It would have been unthinkable a few years ago that employees of whatever grade in, say, hospitals would use the sufferings of the sick to obtain higher cash payments. Bad example is catching, and once established it is difficult to eradicate; but the effort must now be made. Whether the answer lies in legislation forbidding strikes and other industrial action in essential services we do not know, though we doubt whether by itself it would be of much use – note the French air-controllers' go-slow, and the improbability that miners and electricity workers, or firemen and hospital workers, would abstain from strikes and work-to-rule just because an Act of Parliament said they should. Legislation, how-

ever, is important because it can express the general conviction of the community as to the rightness and wrongness of particular behaviour; to be effective, it must be supported by other measures. Long-term measures are basically the most important, such as a re-awakening of the moral sense of those who are involved; but by definition it will take considerable time before these can have any effect, and even then they will not restrain those who are still actuated by envy, greed or sloth.

58. A further and more immediate step is to set up consultative machinery which will be respected, and in which all the interests and issues are made apparent. Bargaining at the moment takes place between employer or paymaster and employee; the social interest, the consumer's interest, the interlocking claims of other members of the society, are not formally represented and are usually totally ignored. New multipartite machinery would meet this need.

59. In addition, if workers in a particular trade are to forgo their legal right to withdraw their labour by striking after due notice, or to abstain from exercising an actual power (though contrary to the law of contract) to take other action such as the go-slow, they must be offered some inducement or compensation, adding up to a fair remuneration for their work. At the same time it may be necessary to consider whether an attempt should be made to limit the effect of their monopoly power. A structure of extra payment for abandonment of the industrial weapon (which would presumably be payable in proportion as the other part of the contract, to abstain from industrial action, was performed) would have to be introduced.

60. Apart from workers with too much muscle, which they exercise to the profound detriment of their fellow-citizens, there are workers with too little muscle. These include most persons in the direct employment of central and local government, as well as many in the caring pro-

fessions. Civil servants, schoolteachers, and the like often have no power to inflict harm on the community at large by industrial action. Though government may suffer if civil servants do not collect taxes, and schoolchildren suffer if teachers do not teach them, the community at large can endure the deprivation (at least in the short term), whereas they find it impossible to resist the cutting off of the electricity supply. Employees in public employment now find themselves the sole target of governmental pay control policies, and see their earnings restricted while employees in other sectors race ahead with large and inflationary wage settlements. The difference in bargaining power made little difference in the days when wage settlements were in single figures or occurred at infrequent intervals – now that double-figure wage settlements are the norm, and the yearly wage-claim is an institution, this means that workers in public employment and in other 'soft' areas are progressively paid less and less compared with other workers.

61. This is not fair, or at least its fairness has not been demonstrated. A just structure for settling claims about pay and conditions of employment must take account of this factor. We must confine ourselves to pointing out the need for such a structure, without investigating in detail what it should be, as this would take us too far away from our theme. It may be that some linking mechanism between industrial and other wages, or some countervailing tax system that would penalise increases over the norm, is the answer: we do not know.